GLACIERS
Ice on the Move

The icy arm of a glacier spreads into a valley.

GLACIERS
Ice on the Move

A Carolrhoda Earth Watch Book

by Sally M. Walker

Carolrhoda Books, Inc./Minneapolis

The author wishes to thank Ross Powell and James A. Walker for reviewing the manuscript through its many stages. And thanks to Margaret Lloyd Robertson and Marybeth Lorbiecki for their work on the manuscript. Also a special thanks to Jean and Thomas Evans for sharing their Camp Century information and experiences.

Thanks to Professor Howard Mooers, Department of Geology, University of Minnesota, for his assistance with this book.

Photo Credits

Photographs courtesy of: front cover, pp. 2, 12, 14, 17, 18, 19, 20, 21, 33, 34, 36, 37, 40, 42, Jay A. Stravers; pp. 5, 30, 45, Ruth Berman; pp. 7, 28, 29, Michael Havrisko; pp. 10, 15, 16, 25, 26, 32, 39, 44, back cover, Ross Powell; p. 23, U.S. Army; p. 35, Ellen A. Cowan

LIBRARY OF CONGRESS CATALOGING-IN-PUBLICATION DATA

Walker, Sally M.
    Glaciers, ice on the move / by Sally M. Walker.
        p.   cm.
    "A Carolrhoda earth watch book."
    Summary: Describes the formation and movement of different types of glaciers, their effects on the land, and how scientists study glaciers.
    ISBN 0-87614-373-7 (lib. bdg.)
    1. Glaciers—Juvenile literature. [1. Glaciers.] I. Title.
GB2403.8.W35   1990
551.3′12—dc20   89-22102
                                                                CIP
                                                                AC

Manufactured in the United States of America

1 2 3 4 5 6 7 8 9 10 99 98 97 96 95 94 93 92 91 90

Over time, glaciers have sculpted these mountains.

Throughout history, glaciers have changed the face of the earth many times. They are slowly changing the face of the earth right now. In Nova Scotia, Canada, a boulder weighing thousands of pounds balances on one edge. Between Nepal and Tibet, in Asia, the sharply carved peak of Mount Everest, the tallest mountain in the world, points toward the sky. At Kelleys Island, in Lake Erie north of Sandusky, Ohio, the rocks are marked with grooves 1 to 2 feet (.3 to .6 m) deep and 2 to 3½ feet (.6 to 1 m) wide. The balanced boulder, the sharp mountain peak, and the deeply grooved rocks are all examples of the power of glaciers—ice on the move.

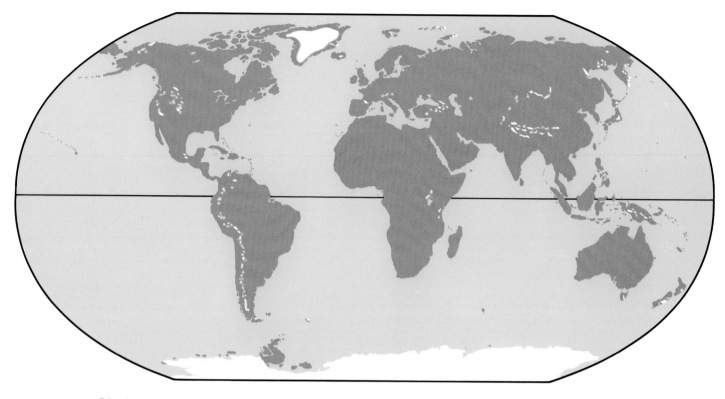

Glaciers are represented by the white areas in this map of the world.

Approximately one-tenth of the earth's surface is covered by glaciers. They exist as giant sheets of ice in polar regions such as Antarctica and parts of Greenland, Iceland, Canada, the Soviet Union, and Alaska. Smaller glaciers are found on tall mountains all over the world. Glaciers hold almost 75 percent of the world's fresh water supply. Arapaho Glacier, in Colorado, with a length and width of about ¾ of a mile (1.2 km), is a small glacier—only one of thousands all over the world. This small glacier alone supplies water for the more than 75,000 people who live in Boulder, Colorado. If all existing glaciers were to melt, world sea levels would rise more than 180 feet (55 m). Coastal cities, like Los Angeles, New York, London, Paris, and Bombay, would be under water. The shapes of all the continents as we know them would change.

Glaciers form in places where the air temperature never gets warm enough to completely melt the snow. Over the years, the snow becomes deeper as new snow falls. Snowflakes are the building blocks that eventually form glaciers.

How do snowflakes become a glacier? Snowflakes are lacy six-sided crystals of frozen water vapor. Like a piece of lace, a snowflake crystal has spaces filled with air. As a matter of fact, snowflakes are 80 percent air. On the ground, snowflakes melt, refreeze, and are pressed into icy, rounded grains. This process begins when air temperatures rise and snowflake crystals start melting. Water from the melted part of the snowflake dribbles toward the center of the crystal and fills some of the air spaces. If the air temperature drops, the melted water refreezes. Then new snow falls on top of the old snow. The weight of the new snow squeezes air from the old snowflakes by breaking off their lacy points and packing them more tightly together. The layers of snow become harder, icier, and more solid.

The same process occurs when a person forms snow into a snowball. As the snowflakes are pressed together, heat from the person's hands partially melts the snow. The crystals are crushed and broken. Some of the air spaces are filled with water, others are squeezed out as the crystals are packed tightly together. The snowball becomes heavier and icier.

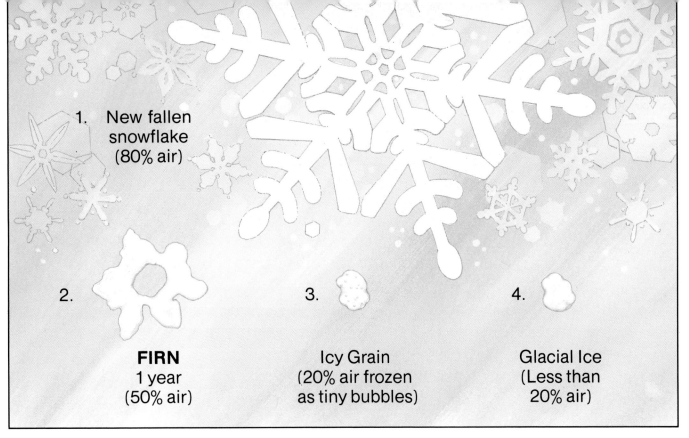

1. New fallen snowflake (80% air)

2. **FIRN**
1 year
(50% air)

3. Icy Grain
(20% air frozen
as tiny bubbles)

4. Glacial Ice
(Less than
20% air)

From snowflake to glacial ice

Snow that has lost 50 percent of its air and that has survived at least one summer without melting completely and turning into ice is called **firn.** The word comes from the Swiss dialect of the German language and means "last year's snow."

Firn becomes glacial ice when the individual rounded icy grains are pressed together until they lock and form a solid mass of ice. Water from melting snowflakes and the pressure caused by increasing layers of snow force almost all of the air from the snow crystals. The air passages inside and between grains of snow are closed off. Some air does not escape during the melting and squeezing process. These pockets of air remain frozen as tiny air bubbles inside glacial ice. The color of glacial ice varies. Air bubbles make glacial ice look white, airless ice is blue.

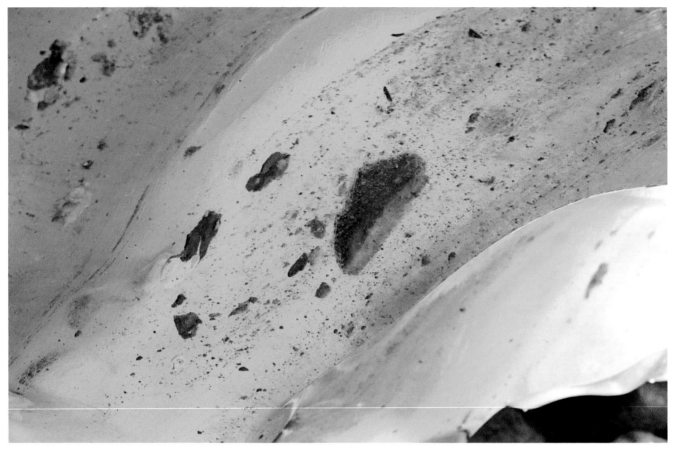

Pebbles trapped within glacial ice

In places like Alaska, where air and snow temperatures allow some melting and new snowfalls to occur often, firn becomes glacial ice within 30 to 50 years—a relatively short time. In Antarctica, this change may take as long as 3,500 years due to the extreme cold and lack of moisture for new snowfall. The gradual change of snowflakes to firn to glacial ice is a continual process. All three forms are part of every glacier.

Glacial ice is a type of rock; the ice crystals are locked together as the result of changes in temperature and pressure. Rocks changed by temperature and pressure are known as **metamorphic rocks**. Glacial ice melts at temperatures far lower than any other rock.

Before glacial ice can be called a glacier, the ice must begin to move. Exactly when a body of ice begins to move depends on how thick and heavy the ice is, the steepness of the glacier's and the earth's surfaces, and the surrounding air temperature. Under the pull of gravity, the ice slowly changes shape and moves. Glaciers do not necessarily move quickly—perhaps only 1 to 2 inches (2.5 to 5 cm) a day.

Runaway Glaciers

While most glaciers move only several feet per year, occasionally they move faster. Sometimes a glacier surges, or flows rapidly, at speeds faster than 100 feet (30 m) a day. The quickly flowing ice in a surging glacier is strong enough to sweep up a boulder as if it were a small stone.

Hubbard Glacier, in Alaska, provided a dramatic example of what can happen when a glacier surges. During the past century, Hubbard Glacier had advanced at a normal glacial speed toward Disenchantment Bay, about 30 miles (48 km) from the city of Yakutat. By 1982, the glacier's snout had extended across the water of the bay, almost closing off the mouth of Russell Fjord. In the spring of 1986, the ice began moving rapidly.

Valerie Glacier, a small glacier that joins with Hubbard near the mouth of Russell Fjord, began surging. It advanced as quickly as 130 feet (40 m) a day. Valerie's forward push caused the snout of Hubbard Glacier to spread farther across the bay. Ice plugged the narrow outlet of Russell Fjord with boulders, mud, and gravel. During the following months, rain and meltwater from Hubbard Glacier built up behind the ice dam. At times, the water level of Russell Fjord, by then a lake, rose 1 foot (.3 m) a day. By early October, the newly formed lake had risen 80 feet (24 m) above sea level. Finally, on October 9, 1987, the massive ice dam broke. Waves of water gushed out in 35 mph (56 kph) bursts. Wave heights reached 30 feet (9 m) and swept ice and rock into the bay. Scientists observing the break said the ice and water roared and boomed as the dam broke up.

The reasons that glaciers surge are not clearly understood. Usually meltwater drains away from glaciers through cracks and tunnels in the ice. If the cracks become clogged, water does not drain away and may build up beneath the ice. This buildup of water reduces the friction between the ice and the underlying rock, allowing the glacier to slide swiftly. Geologists are still looking for the complete answer as to why glaciers surge.

These grooves at Kelleys Island were gouged into the rock by the movements of a glacier.

Glaciers move in two ways, by **basal sliding** and by **plastic flow**. Basal sliding occurs when a layer of water or of water-soaked **sediment** (very small pieces of rock) is present at the base, or bottom, of a glacier. The layer of water or of water-soaked sediment, sometimes no thicker than a sheet of construction paper, allows the glacier to slide over the rock surface below. The water beneath a glacier forms when ice is melted by the earth's heat and by the heat produced from friction. Friction is created when two objects rub against each other. As ice scrapes against the earth's surface, it creates friction, which produces enough heat to melt some of the ice on the bottom of the glacier. In addition to producing heat, friction slows the movement of the whole glacier.

Basal sliding occurs along the bottom of a glacier. In the past, the only way scientists knew that the sliding occurred was because the ice left scratches and grooves in the underlying rock after the ice melted away. Now glaciologists, scientists who study glaciers, use special machinery to dig tunnels into the side of a glacier so they can actually watch the movement.

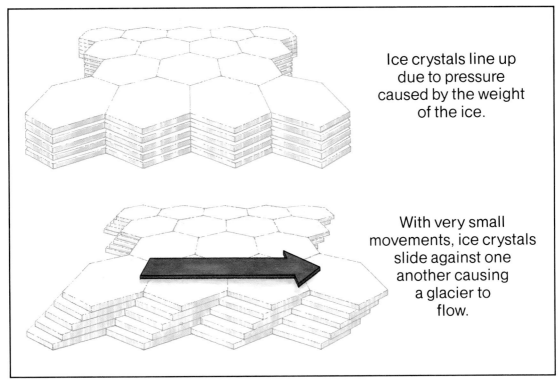

Ice crystals line up due to pressure caused by the weight of the ice.

With very small movements, ice crystals slide against one another causing a glacier to flow.

The movement of ice crystals in a glacier during plastic flow

Plastic flow, the other way glaciers move, occurs inside a glacier and is a result of great pressure. The tremendous weight of the ice forces individual ice crystals to line up in such a way that they slide against one another. These very small, continuous movements cause the ice to bend and flow.

Ice and other material undergoing plastic flow do not snap back into their original shape after the pressure is removed. The new shape remains until additional pressure changes it. Soft Play Dough and Silly Putty are plastic materials. They bend and flow easily from the pressure applied by a person's hands. Ice deep inside a glacier acts like a plastic material.

All glaciers move by basal sliding and by plastic flow. Very large glaciers, however, move more by plastic flow than by basal sliding, because they are so thick and heavy.

Several valley glaciers often combine to form a larger glacier.

Glaciers move at different speeds. Glaciers on steep slopes flow faster than those on level ground. The thicker the ice, the more likely glaciers are to move on level ground because the weight of the ice forces greater plastic flow. Very thick ice can actually move uphill as it flows across land. A glacier in an extremely cold region may flow at a slower rate than a glacier in warmer regions, since the temperature of the ice would prevent some basal melting from occurring.

In the nineteenth century, a scientist named Louis Agassiz (LOO-ee AH-guh-see) carried out an experiment that showed that the center of a glacier moves more quickly than the sides. He drilled a line of holes across the surface of a glacier that was flowing through a valley in Switerland, put a stake in each hole, and left them. When Agassiz returned months later, he found that the stakes inserted in the central holes had traveled farther down the valley than the stakes inserted near the valley walls.

These men must be careful not to get too close to the crevasse because crevasses may be many feet deep.

Friction between a glacier and the surrounding valley walls slows the ice flow along a glacier's edges.

Ice near the surface is very brittle. When a glacier flows over uneven land, the surface ice may crack, unlike the ice deep inside a glacier, which bends. These cracks, or **crevasses** (kreh-VAHS-ez), can be very wide and may be as deep as 150 to 200 feet (46 to 61 m). Often they are hidden by a thin layer of snow and are difficult to see. This makes walking across a glacier dangerous.

Ice is calving from the front of Taylor Glacier, in Antarctica.

Glaciers continually gain and lose ice. New snow is added to a glacier in an area called the **zone of accumulation**. In this area more snow and ice accumulate during the winter than melt during the summer. A glacier continues growing larger as new snow falls.

The area where glaciers lose snow and ice is called the **zone of ablation**. Loss of snow and ice in glaciers is usually caused by melting or by melting followed by evaporation, the change of liquid water into water vapor. Glaciers can also lose snow by **sublimation**, a process during which snow changes directly from a solid into water vapor without first melting. Sublimation usually occurs in places where the temperature is below the freezing point, so very little melting occurs. If a glacier's front, or **snout**, ends in a body of water, large chunks of ice will break off the snout and float away. When this happens, the glacier is said to be **calving**.

A glacier advances, or grows larger, when new snow is added at a faster rate than it is lost. If snow and ice are lost faster than they accumulate, the glacier retreats, or becomes smaller. This doesn't mean that the ice flows backward. Rather, the glacier's size is reduced by melting, sublimation, calving, or a combination of all three. If accumulation and ablation are equal, a glacier stays the same size. However, the glacier continues to flow forward.

At one time, this valley glacier reached the water. When snow and ice melted faster than they accumulated, the glacier retreated from the water.

Snow collects in this mountain cirque.

There are two main types of glacier—**valley glaciers** and **ice sheets**. Valley glaciers begin their formation on mountains. Snow collects on the sides of mountains in bowl-shaped depressions called **cirques** (serks). As snow and ice seep into cracks in the cirque, they partially melt and refreeze. Ice expands when it freezes and acts like a wedge inside the cracks. Pieces of rock are chipped from the cirque walls by the expanding ice, enlarging the bowl shape. The ice continues to accumulate until it finally spills over the cirque edge and flows downhill into the valley below.

Valley glaciers are also called rivers of ice because they follow paths that were originally formed by rivers. When two or more valley glaciers flow into a large valley, they squeeze together. Glaciers do not intermix the way water streams would because ice is solid. Several valley glaciers often combine to form a larger glacier.

A piedmont glacier's movement is slowed as it spreads onto a plain. Fjords can be seen in the distance.

Valley glaciers vary in length according to their location and the amount of snowfall they receive. One well-known valley glacier in Alaska, Hubbard Glacier, is over 200 miles (322 km) long. But most valley glaciers are less than 2 miles (3.2 km) long.

When one or more valley glaciers flow through a narrow valley down to a wide lowland area, like a plain, the ice spreads. This large, fan-shaped glacier is called a **piedmont glacier**. The long, thin handle of the fan carries new ice onto the plain. The glacier's movement is slowed as the ice spreads over the large area. Friction between the ice and the rocky plain also slows the glacier's movement.

Nunataks are mountaintops that poke through thick ice sheets.

Ice sheets, the other main type of glacier, are the world's largest glaciers. In areas where the air temperature never rises above 32° F (0° C), very little melting occurs. The continued addition of new snow gradually forms layer upon layer of glacial ice, which becomes a thick, slow-moving ice blanket. The thick ice, called an ice sheet, flows over large areas of land and is so deep only the tallest mountaintops poke above it. These mountain peaks are called **nunataks** (NUHN-uh-tahks). The name comes from an Inuit word meaning "island in a sea of ice."

Today ice sheets exist in Greenland and Antarctica. They account for about 95 percent of the world's glacial ice. Greenland is covered by one ice sheet that is more than 1 mile (1.6 km) deep in spots. Two ice sheets cover Antarctica. The East Antarctic Ice Sheet is the larger one, covering more than half of the continent. The West Antarctic Ice Sheet covers part of the continent and some islands along the coast.

The ice sheet that covers Greenland is more than 1 mile (1.6 km) deep in spots.

A City Inside the Ice

In 1959 and 1960, the United States government sent a group of army engineers to Greenland. Their job was to build a city inside the ice sheet. The city, named Camp Century, would serve two purposes. One was to protect the United States in case of attack; missiles could be hidden in tunnels inside the ice. The other purpose was to gather information about glaciers and about living in extremely cold environments.

Special plows cut rooms into the thick ice. Tunnels connected groups of rooms. Corrugated steel arches lined the ceilings to prevent melting and for support. Soldiers were stationed at Camp Century for several months at a time. They called themselves "ice worms."

After the army personnel left Camp Century, scientists came to study the ice, searching for clues about Greenland's past natural history. Each year, new snow pressed Camp Century about 1½ feet (.46 m) deeper into the ice. The walls also pressed inward. Because ice as thick as the Greenland Ice Sheet moves so slowly, the scientists were not worried about the ceilings caving in. The biggest problem was the ongoing process of digging down into the camp as new snow accumulated. Eventually, digging through the deep snow to reach the camp became too difficult. The camp, no longer used, has been buried by many feet of ice and has probably collapsed.

Workers at Camp Century, Greenland, install steel arches over a trench as they build a city inside the ice sheet.

Ice sheets are so heavy they actually cause the underlying rock to sink into the earth. The earth's surface beneath ice sheets has been pushed hundreds of feet below sea level. After the ice melts, the earth's surface will rise again, like a spongy cake, but may take many thousands of years. In North America, the land north of the Great Lakes and parts of New England have been rising since the melting away of an ice sheet that covered much of the northern portion of the continent more than 10,000 years ago.

The thickness of ice sheets can be measured with a seismograph, an instrument used to measure earthquake waves. Holes are drilled into the ice and dynamite charges are exploded inside them, sending vibrations, or waves, through the ice. The waves travel through the glacial ice until they reach the land surface below. Because the surface below is a different type of rock than glacial ice, the waves are reflected back toward the seismograph. Glaciologists know that the waves move through glacial ice at certain speeds. By recording the amount of time the waves take to bounce back to the seismograph, glaciologists can calculate the distance the waves have traveled and therefore the thickness of the ice sheet.

Glaciologists also use radio waves to measure ice depth. This method works in much the same way as measuring with a seismograph. Since radio waves can be sent from airplanes, they are particularly useful for measuring the ice depth of large areas that are covered by ice sheets. When glaciologists first collected information from radio wave measurements of the Antarctic ice sheets, they discovered that the ice sheets completely cover mountains that had not been known to exist. Radio waves have enabled glaciologists to calculate that the Antarctic ice sheets are, in some places, greater than 15,000 feet (4,572 m) deep.

Seismograph and radio waves have helped scientists draw topographical maps, detailed maps of land surface elevations. With these maps we can "see" what the Antarctic land surface looks like beneath its thick ice cover.

The Ross Ice Shelf, in Antarctica, is the size of Texas and is hundreds of feet thick.

When an ice sheet extends into the sea, it forms a floating **ice shelf**, which is connected to land on one side. This extension into the sea ends in a steep cliff, which forms when chunks of ice calve off the front of the ice shelf and float away. These cliffs often tower hundreds of feet above the water. Ice shelves also extend many more hundreds of feet below the water's surface.

Only about one-tenth of this iceberg is visible. The rest of the iceberg is hidden under water.

All glaciers that meet the sea calve, producing icebergs. Although icebergs often look small when viewed from the water's surface, they may be huge. Since icebergs are slightly lighter than water, they float. Only one-tenth to one-eighth of an iceberg sticks out of the water. Some icebergs rise 400 feet (122 m) above the ocean. That's taller than a 30-story apartment building! But the part of the iceberg beneath the water's surface may reach a depth of 2,800 feet (853 m)—two times the height of the world's tallest skyscraper.

Sometimes large, flat blocks of ice calve off an ice sheet. These

Floating Danger

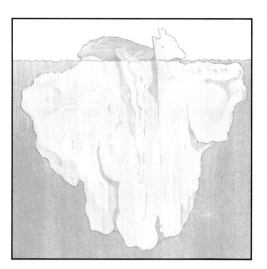

Hundreds of icebergs calve off the Greenland Ice Sheet each year. They can cause great danger to ships. On April 12, 1912, a brand-new ocean liner, the *Titanic*, left England on a voyage to New York City. The ship's owners said she was unsinkable. During the night of April 14, the *Titanic* struck an iceberg. Ice pushed in her steel sides and gouged at least one hole. Water rushed into the ship's hold. The ship sank in less than three hours. Over 1,500 of the more than 2,200 people on board, some of them children, died in the freezing water.

Recently, scientists from the United States used a minisubmarine and a specially built robot camera to locate and explore the wreckage of the mighty ship. They have not yet been able to determine exactly how the ice destroyed the *Titanic*, only that it did.

Partly as a result of the *Titanic* disaster, a special International Ice Patrol was established. United States Coast Guard boats carefully watch the waters of the North Atlantic Ocean. Airplane pilots spot icebergs and radio in their locations. The ice patrol alerts ships in the area. Many potentially terrible accidents have been avoided due to the hard work of the ice patrol.

floating islands can be miles long and hold enormous amounts of fresh water—in the form of ice, of course. Scientists believe that towing some of these large icebergs to dry countries would be possible. Although some of the ice would melt, if the iceberg were protected with layers of plastic, enough ice would remain to supply plenty of water for desert agriculture. Once the iceberg reached its destination, the ice could be melted and transported through pipes to the areas where water was needed. Maybe this will happen during your lifetime.

The Matterhorn

The movement of glaciers across the earth's surface dramatically changes the land's appearance. The Grand Teton Mountains, in the western United States, and the Alps, in Europe, were sculpted by ice. Glaciers continually enlarge cirques on mountaintops. Sometimes several cirques form on one mountain, shaping the top into a sharp peak. These sharp peaks, called **horns**, are found in many mountain ranges. The Matterhorn, in Switzerland, is a famous example of a horn.

A valley's shape is changed by the action of a glacier. As ice grinds against the walls and floor of a narrow, V-shaped valley, the rock below is worn away, forming glacial valleys that are broad and U-shaped. Rocks picked up and carried along by the glacier often scrape long scratches, called **striations**, into the valley floor and walls.

Glacially molded hills and fjords can be seen in Kragerø, Norway.

Land surface changes caused by glaciers along a coastline are often spectacular. Thousands of people tour the coastal waters of Norway each year. They go to admire the majestic beauty of the glacially molded hills beside the sea. The waterways, or **fjords** (fee-ORDS), that their ships cruise on are actually underwater valleys dug by glaciers! At one time, glaciers flowed beyond the coastline and gouged the ocean floor. After the glaciers retreated to the coastline, seawater flooded the deep trenches. Sogne Fjord, 45 miles (72 km) north of Bergen, Norway, is 4,080 feet (1,244 m) deep at its mouth. Fjords are also found along the coasts of Alaska, Chile, New Zealand, and western Canada.

The Great Lakes, in the north-central United States, were formed by ice sheet movement. At various times throughout the Pleistocene (PLYS-tuh-seen) Epoch, ice flowed over the region and gouged the land, forming a series of basins. Later, as the ice melted, the basins filled with meltwater from the ice sheet and rain. Glacial ice floated in the Great Lakes as recently as 10,000 years ago.

Rock material carried by glaciers to areas far from their source are called **erratics** and can range in size from a pebble to a boulder. Fossils, the naturally preserved remains of plants and animals, are also carried to areas far from their source. The area over which a glacier has traveled, and the direction in which the ice has moved may be determined by the kind of rocks and fossils the ice has deposited.

The moraine in front of this glacier was formed when ice pushed sediment into the shape of a hill.

Till, a mixture of soil and rocks carried and deposited by glaciers, also changes the shape of the landscape. Glaciers, acting like giant bulldozers, push till into ridgelike deposits called **moraines**. Moraines form along the sides and front of a glacier. When two glaciers flow beside each other, both depositing rocks, a moraine is formed between them. Moraines in these areas appear as dark lines on the surface of the ice. Long Island, New York, is a moraine deposited during the most recent glacial period, about 15,000 years ago. Much of the rock material that forms Long Island was carried by glaciers from areas in the Appalachian Mountains, in northern New England.

This drumlin field is in the state of New York.

Drumlins are another type of hill formed by glaciers. Glaciologists are not sure how drumlins form. Some glaciologists believe they form when an ice sheet scrapes away till that was deposited by earlier ice sheets, leaving behind spoon-shaped hills of more resistant till. Others think drumlins are deposited onto the land surface by melted water flowing beneath the glacier. A third group believes drumlins form in both ways. The Battle of Bunker Hill, a famous American Revolutionary War battle, was fought on a drumlin that was formed during the same glacial period that Long Island was formed.

Meltwater streaming away from a glacier deposits **outwash**,

An outwash plain in Alaska is crisscrossed by meltwater streams.

sediment that has washed out from the ice. Outwash has a more layered appearance than till because sediment deposited by water settles according to particle size. Large pieces of rock are heavy and settle quickly. Fine sediment remains suspended in the water for a longer period of time because it is lightweight. **Rock flour**, a very finely ground, powdery rock material, often gives meltwater a milky appearance. Because rock flour is the lightest glacially ground rock, it is carried and deposited farther from the glacier than larger, heavier rocks.

An esker, winding from top to bottom, can be seen at the right of this photograph. The esker is surrounded by water-filled kettles.

Eskers are long, snaky ridges of outwash sediment. Meltwater streams, flowing inside cracks and beneath melting glaciers, create winding tunnels. As water flows through the tunnels, sediment is deposited. A long, winding esker is left after all the ice has melted.

Kettles are bowl-shaped areas in the ground that are formed when blocks of ice are buried in outwash sediment. After the glacier retreats, the buried ice block melts. A hole is left in its place. Kettles range in size from a few feet across to several hundred feet across. Some kettles fill with meltwater and rain, forming lakes. In the United States, many kettle lakes can be found in Minnesota and Wisconsin.

If you live in an area once covered by ice, there may be glacial landforms in or near your town. Many of the gravel pits that supply stone for concrete are excavated glacial landforms.

Glaciers have covered great portions of the earth at least six times during the past 960 million years. Those periods of time are called ice ages. The most recent large-scale ice age occurred during the Pleistocene Epoch, a geologic time period that began approximately 2 million years ago and lasted until 10 thousand years ago. In the past, scientists believed ice sheets advanced 4 times during the Pleistocene. Now, evidence from sediment cores drilled along the bottoms of the Atlantic and Pacific Oceans indicates ice sheets advanced at least as many as 20 times over parts of North America, Europe, and Asia. Grouped together, these advances are called the Great Ice Age. In the United States, the last major glacial advance is called the Wisconsin, named after the area where its glacial landforms are best described.

Outwash deposits like these are often gravel rich.

The climate did not always remain cold during the Great Ice Age. The ice sheet advances were separated by very warm periods of time lasting several thousand years. During some of the warm periods, there were fewer glaciers than there are today. Scientists believe that the alternation of very cold and very warm periods is caused by changes in the earth's orbit, or path, around the sun. Sometimes, the earth is farther from and tilted away from the sun. At these times, the earth is cool, so large glaciers can develop. Other times, the earth is closer to and tilted toward the sun. At these times, the earth is much warmer, so fewer glaciers will form. Cores drilled from sediment found deep in the ocean floors provide evidence that the cold and warm periods of the Great Ice Age match the changes in the earth's orbit during these time periods.

During the Great Ice Age, ice covered as much as 30 percent of the earth's surface. If you could have visited the areas where New England and the north-central states are now, you would have found them covered by thick ice. In Europe, one ice sheet spread into central Germany and Poland, as far south as the Baltic Sea, and as far west as Moscow, in the Soviet Union.

Studying the Ice

A number of nations have polar research laboratories in Antarctica, where scientists study the ice. Using special drills, geologists take samples of the ice sheets. The drills dig out cores, long pipe-shaped sections of ice. As the drills cut into the ice, they reach older and older layers of ice. Volcanic dust found in these layers provides information about some ancient geological events. Pollen and other plant remains found in cores drilled in outwash can give us clues as to what plant life existed and what climates were like thousands of years ago.

Scientists also observe what happens when ice meets the sea. Sometimes large pieces of ice break off of an ice sheet. Bits of rock, frozen inside the ice, gradually fall off and settle to the ocean floor as the ice drifts and melts. The trail of rocks across the ocean floor can help scientists understand how ocean currents move.

A geologist collects samples inside an ice cave.

A large amount of the earth's water was frozen in ice sheets, so the Pleistocene sea levels were much lower than they are today. Because of the lower sea levels, a bridge of land stretched between Asia and Alaska. For thousands of years, this land bridge allowed animals to roam freely between the two continents. Woolly mammoths and mastodons crossed into North America on the land bridge, as did buffalo. It is probable that humans may have arrived in North America by crossing the land bridge.

Why do ice ages occur? There are many theories, or explanations based on scientific study and reasoning, that try to answer this question.

Many scientists believe that the position of the continents in or near polar regions is necessary for the development of an ice age. Polar regions are colder than the rest of the earth's surface because they receive less solar radiation. If the average air temperature above a continent is lowered, ice sheets can develop. Antarctica is an example of what can happen on a continent in or near polar regions.

Meltwater is streaming off the snout of this glacier.

Oceans also hold a key to ice-age development. Ocean waters can be warm or cold, depending on their depth (the deeper the water, the colder it is) and location on the earth. Near the equator, the area of the earth that is equally distant to the North and South Poles, ocean water is warm because it receives the most solar radiation. If this warm water circulates freely into polar regions, the air temperature at the poles will be warmer. In addition, the water's dark color absorbs more solar radiation than the lighter color of the land surface. This warms the air above the water even more, so an ice age is less likely to occur. When continental landmasses are near polar regions, they become a barrier preventing warm ocean currents from reaching polar areas. As a result, the air temperature is colder, favoring the development of an ice age.

What would happen to the glaciers on earth right now if average air temperatures became warmer? Scientists are now watching the slight increase in worldwide temperatures that is due, in part, to the **greenhouse effect.** This warming trend is caused by the sun and certain gases in the earth's atmosphere. Scientists are concerned about the increasing levels of two gases in particular—chlorofluoro-carbons (called CFCs for short) and carbon dioxide. CFCs are produced during some manufacturing processes. Carbon dioxide occurs naturally in the earth's atmosphere, but the amount in the atmosphere is greatly increased by people when we burn oil, gas, coal, and forestlands.

Heat from the sun warms the earth's surface. Normally this heat is radiated back into space as **infrared energy**, a form of energy composed of heat rays that are not visible to human eyes. Carbon dioxide and CFCs in the earth's atmosphere absorb some of the infrared energy, keeping it in the earth's atmosphere. This causes air temperatures to rise.

A small whisper of a glacier lies on a beach. If average temperatures become warmer, water that had been stored in glaciers would slowly flood coastal cities all over the world.

The U.S. National Academy of Science predicts average worldwide temperatures may rise anywhere from 2.7° to 8.1° F (about 1.5° to 5° C) over the next 50 to 100 years as a result of the greenhouse effect. An average increase of only about 2° F (about 1° C) is enough to increase the melting of the world's glaciers. If average air temperatures become warmer, present sea levels could rise as much as 28 inches (71 cm) and slowly flood the world's coastal cities. Scientists, manufacturers, political leaders, and others are working together to learn more about the greenhouse effect, so we can take steps toward solving this problem.

A glacial river streams through the valley city of Chamonix, France.

Will there be another ice age? Geologists are not in agreement. Scientists must continue to study glaciers to better understand how they affect our climate. They must determine what controls ice speed, surging, and iceberg calving rates. They need to examine what effects large-scale glacial melting would have on the earth and on the plants and animals living here. Only further study can give glaciologists the information they need to predict accurately what glaciers may do in the future.

GLOSSARY

basal sliding: the movement of a glacier that depends on the pull of gravity and on a thin layer of water between glacier and land

calving: ice chunks breaking off the front of glaciers that end in a body of water

cirques: bowl-shaped depressions that may be left on mountains after glaciers have melted

crevasses: large cracks that may form in the brittle surface of glaciers

drumlins: spoon-shaped hills of glacial sediment

erratics: rocks carried away from their original resting places by glaciers

eskers: long, winding ridges of sediment deposited by meltwater streams that flowed in tunnels within, or under glaciers

firn: snowflakes that have lost half their air and that have not completely melted during their first summer

fjords: valleys dug by glaciers that flow beyond the coastline and gouge the ocean floor

greenhouse effect: a warming of the earth caused by the sun's rays heating certain gases in the earth's atmosphere

horns: peaks shaped by glaciers that have carved a mountaintop on two or more sides

ice sheets: very thick, slow-moving glaciers that cover large areas of a continent

ice shelf: an ice sheet that is connected to land on one side and ends in a steep cliff over a body of water on the other side

infrared energy: invisible heat rays that are produced by objects

kettles: bowl-shaped areas in the ground that form after blocks of ice have been buried in outwash sediment and have melted. Some kettles fill with water and become lakes.

metamorphic rocks: rocks that are changed by temperature and pressure

moraines: deposits of glacial till that have been pushed into a hill shape by glaciers

nunataks: tall mountain peaks that poke through ice sheets

outwash: sediment that is sorted according to size then deposited by meltwater streaming away from a glacier

piedmont glacier: a large, fan-shaped glacier that forms when one or more valley glaciers flow into a wide lowland area

plastic flow: a way for a glacier to move that occurs inside a glacier and is the result of enormous pressure

rock flour: the powder from rocks that are finely ground by the movement of glaciers

sediment: bits and pieces of rock and soil deposited by water, wind, or glaciers

snout: the front of a glacier

striations: scratches carved into hard earth surfaces by rocks that were dragged by glaciers

sublimation: the evaporation of a solid into vapor without it undergoing the middle stage of melting

till: rock material deposited directly by melting glaciers

valley glaciers: glaciers that begin on mountains, flow downhill, and often follow paths that were originally formed by rivers

zone of ablation: the area where snow and ice are lost by a glacier

zone of accumulation: the area where new snow is added to a glacier

INDEX

ABOUT THE AUTHOR

Sally M. Walker earned her B.A. degree in Physics and Planetary Sciences at Upsala College, in New Jersey. She now lives in Illinois with her husband and two children. She writes during times snatched between volunteer work at her children's school and a thousand and one daily errands. When she writes, Ms. Walker is assisted by her cat, who sits on the desk next to the typewriter, and her golden retriever, who wedges herself between Ms. Walker's feet and takes a nap.